Friends to the End for Kids

Other Books by Bradley Trevor Greive

The Blue Day Book

The Blue Day Book for Kids

The Blue Day Journal and Directory

Dear Mom

Looking for Mr. Right

The Meaning of Life

The Incredible Truth About Mothers

Tomorrow

Priceless: The Vanishing Beauty of a Fragile Planet

The Book for People Who Do Too Much

Friends to the End

Dear Dad

The Simple Truth About Love

Friends to the End
for Kids

The True Value of Friendship

BRADLEY TREVOR GREIVE

Andrews McMeel
Publishing

Kansas City

Friends to the End
for Kids

Trying to talk about our friendship is like chewing
ten pieces of bubble gum at the same time—
it ties my tongue up in knots.

It's really hard to get out
all the words to explain how good it feels
to be your friend,

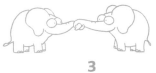

which is pretty weird, because talking
is one of the things we do best.

4

But lately I've been thinking a lot
about friendship

and about what makes it so great
to have good friends.

For one thing,
friends truly care about each other.

You can trust them
with your most secret secrets,

and you can count on them to watch your back

**and never forget about you
or leave you behind.**

It's kind of spooky, but friends
just seem to know what you need
without even saying a word,

whether it's a big hug,

an emergency back scratch,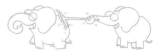

or just a little peace and quiet
to get your thoughts together.

Of course, it's also good to have some
time alone with your favorite toys

15

 or a pig-out snack attack.

But when a friend calls,

you slam on the brakes, turn around,

and then come running
as fast as you can.

Because with friends (and this is the best
thing about friendship), spending time
with each other means fun—loads of fun!

It might mean putting on a hilarious
musical production in fancy costumes

or splashing around in the pool
or at the beach on a hot day.

Friends have fun going on
crazy adventures,

catching the first summer raindrops or
winter snowflakes on the tips of their tongues,

and singing (or screaming at the top of
their lungs) all the words to their favorite songs.

One day you might start out inventing strange, delicious cookies in the kitchen

and end up doing wild and crazy dances
till you are absolutely wiped out.

Of course, every friendship has rough spots, too.

There will be times when we don't see eye-to-eye.
Big arguments can start over silly things.

We might even make the mistake
of letting others come between us.
And that would make me sad.

The truth is that even the best friends
can drive each other crazy from time to time

or do things that are way too gross to believe.

But eventually, we have to shrug our shoulders,
forgive each other, and move on,

because that's what real friends do.

Without friends, life would be
awfully lonely, perhaps a little bit scary,
and certainly a lot more boring.

 After all, you can't do high-fives with yourself
without looking like an idiot.

Sometimes even really fun things
don't seem worth doing
without someone to share them with

and, what's more, with friends we can do
so many things that we just can't do by ourselves.
In fact, with their help, even the
utterly impossible
seems deliciously doable.

True friends make us smile as soon as we see them.

They brighten up our day without even trying—
it just feels good to have them around.

I know how lucky I am
to have found a friend like you.

 And I just want to say that no matter what happens,
you will never be alone,

because I will always be your friend.

Always.